Bengal Tiger

Louise and Richard Spilsbury

Heinemann Library
Chicago, Illinois

Customer Service 888–454–2279

Visit our website at www.heinemannlibrary.com

Photo research by Hannah Taylor and Fiona Orbell
Designed by Michelle Lisseter and Ron Kamen
Printed in China, by South China Printing Co. Ltd.

10 09 08 07 06
10 9 8 7 6 5 4 3 2 1

Library of Congress Cataloging-in-Publication Data
Spilsbury, Louise.
Save the Bengal tiger / Louise and Richard Spilsbury.
     p. cm. -- (Save our animals!)
Includes bibliographical references and index.
ISBN 1-4034-7803-1 (library binding-hardcover) -- ISBN 1-4034-7811-2 (pbk.)
    1. Tigers--Juvenile literature. 2. Tigers--Conservation--Juvenile
literature. I. Spilsbury, Richard, 1963- II. Title. III. Series.

QL737.C23S584 2006
599.756--dc22

                          2005027451

Acknowledgments
The author and publisher are grateful to the following for permission to reproduce copyright material: Ardea pp. **4** top (Y A Betrand), **5** top left, **14** (J Rajput), **16** (P Morris), **28** (J Daniels); Corbis/Gallo Images p. **29** (M Harvey); Digital Vision p. **5** middle; Ecoscene p. **10** (R Gill); FLPA p. **21** (M Newman); Getty Images/National Geographic pp. **26–27** (J Edwards); Naturepl.com pp. **4** bottom left (M Carwardine), **9** (F Savigny), **17** (K Ammann), **23** (M Birkhead); NHPA p. **25** (M Harvey); Oxford Scientific pp. **4** middle, **5** top right, **6**, **7** (M Powles), **11** (M Hill), **13**, **22**; Panos Pictures p. **18** (A Vitale), **19** (Animals Animals); Reuters p. **12** (D Balibouse); Still Pictures pp. **5** bottom, **15** (A & S Carey); WWF-Canon p. **24** (M Harvey).

Cover photograph of Bengal tiger reproduced with permission of Alamy Images/Mike Hill.

The publishers would like to thank Sarala Khaling at WWF in Nepal for her assistance in the preparation of this book.

Every effort has been made to contact copyright holders of any material reproduced in this book. Any omissions will be rectified in subsequent printings if notice is given to the publisher.

Some words are shown in bold, **like this**. You can find out what they mean by looking in the glossary.

Contents

Animals in Trouble

There are many different types, or **species**, of animals. Some species are in danger of becoming **extinct**. This means that all the animals from that species might die.

All the animals shown here
are in danger of becoming
extinct. These species need
to be saved. The Bengal
tiger is one of them.

The Bengal Tiger

Bengal tigers are big animals, but they can be hard to spot. The dark stripes on their orange and white hair help them hide in long, brown grass.

It is hard to spot a Bengal tiger in the grass.

Each Bengal tiger has a different pattern of stripes.

Bengal tigers belong to the cat family. Lions, leopards, and cheetahs also belong to this family. They all have long tails, big teeth, sharp claws, and loud roars.

Where Can You Find Bengal Tigers?

You have to travel to **Asia** to find Bengal tigers. Asia is a **continent**. Most Bengal tigers live in parts of India. A few live in other countries nearby.

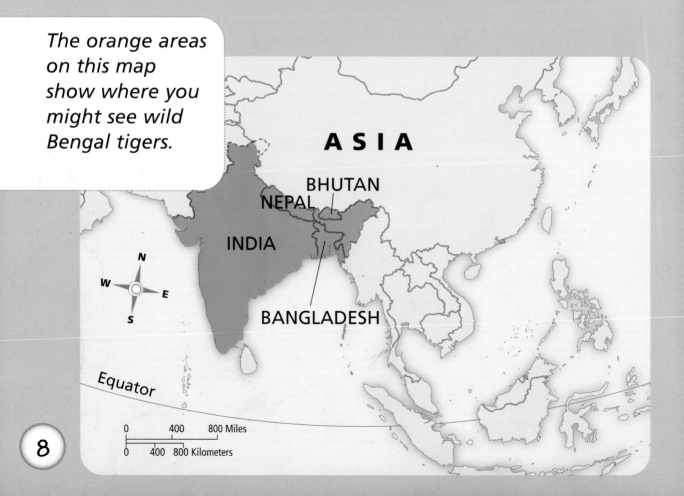

The orange areas on this map show where you might see wild Bengal tigers.

ASIA

BHUTAN

NEPAL

INDIA

BANGLADESH

N
W E
S

Equator

0   400   800 Miles
0   400   800 Kilometers

Where an animal lives is called its **habitat**. Most Bengal tiger habitat is forests or areas with long grass. Tigers can hide there while they hunt for food.

Bengal tigers live in wild places, away from people.

What Do Bengal Tigers Eat?

Bengal tigers are **carnivores**, which means they eat meat. Bengal tigers usually hunt pigs, deer, antelopes, or buffalo.

Tigers have sharp teeth for eating meat.

Tigers need to hunt other animals so that they can eat.

Bengal tigers can hear and see very well. This helps them hunt. A tiger creeps up close behind an animal. Then the tiger runs out to catch it.

Young Bengal Tigers

Baby tigers are called **cubs**. **Female** tigers usually have three or four cubs at a time. They give birth in safe places, such as caves.

Tiger cubs are born with their eyes closed.

Bengal tigers are **mammals**. The cubs feed on their mother's milk. Later their mother will teach them to hunt. After they are two years old, tigers live alone.

Tiger cubs learn hunting skills by playing with each other.

Natural Dangers

Tiger **cubs** face dangers in the wild. Hyenas, leopards, and wild dogs can kill them. Some young tigers die because they cannot catch enough food.

Leopards can catch and eat Bengal tiger cubs.

Adult tigers can protect themselves against most animals.

No wild animals hunt adult Bengal tigers. Adult tigers are too big and strong. They die when they get old or hurt in a fight with another tiger.

Hunting and Poaching

In the past, people enjoyed hunting Bengal tigers. Indian kings and hunters from Europe rode elephants through the forests. They killed thousands of tigers.

Hunters had photos taken to prove they had killed a tiger.

Poachers hunt tigers and other big cats for their skin.

Today it is against the law to kill Bengal tigers, but some people, called **poachers**, still do. They sell tiger skins and bones for a lot of money.

Dangers to the Bengal Tiger's World

People cut down trees in the tigers' **habitat**. They build homes and farms on the land, so there is no room for the tigers or the animals they eat.

When people move to wild places like this, tigers lose their homes.

There can be problems when people live near tigers. Tigers sometimes hunt farm animals. People chase the tigers away. Sometimes they kill the tigers.

These men are carrying sticks to scare tigers away from their town.

How Many Bengal Tigers Are There?

In 1900 there were around 100,000 Bengal tigers in **Asia**. Today there are only about 4,000 left. The problem is that tigers live alone, in small areas.

Year

1900

2005

 = 20,000

This graph shows how many Bengal tigers there are.

People have built towns and roads in these areas. Now it is hard for tigers to find food or travel to meet another tiger to **mate**.

People need to keep wild places for tigers to live in.

How Are Bengal Tigers Being Saved?

Some countries have areas of land called **reserves** where tigers are safe and their **habitat** is looked after. People can come and see tigers in reserves.

People pay to visit tigers in reserves. The money pays for guards, who protect the tigers.

There are laws to stop people from buying and selling Bengal tiger skins and bones. Police catch **poachers** and punish them for harming Bengal tigers.

These are tiger skins that police took from poachers.

Who Is Helping Bengal Tigers?

Groups of people collect money to pay for Bengal tiger **reserves**. They try to stop people from buying medicines made from tiger parts.

Children in school learn how to help save the tigers.

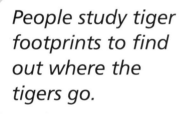

People study tiger footprints to find out where the tigers go.

Some people put radios on tiger collars. These collars show how far tigers travel. Then people know how big the reserves need to be to keep the tigers safe.

How Can You Help?

It is important to know that Bengal tigers are in danger. Then you can learn how to help save them. Read, watch, and find out all you can about Bengal tigers.

Here are some things you can do to help.

- Join a group, such as **WWF**. These groups raise money to protect tigers.
- Visit zoos where tigers live. Some zoos raise money to help wild tigers.

The Future for Bengal Tigers

The future of the Bengal tiger is uncertain. Some people say that there may be none left in the wild by 2010. Then the only ones we see will be in zoos.

Today there are around 300 Bengal tigers in zoos.

We must all work so that Bengal tigers can live free, like this.

Countries must work together to stop people from buying and selling parts of dead tigers. If they are protected, the number of Bengal tigers will grow again.

Bengal Tiger Facts

- Bengal tigers live to be about 15 years old in the wild.
- A tiger can eat more than your weight in meat in one meal.
- No two tigers have the same stripe patterns. Each tiger's stripes are different.
- There are about 40 white Bengal tigers in zoos across the world. They have cream colored fur, chocolate colored stripes, and blue eyes.

Find Out More

Eckart, Edana. *Bengal Tiger*. Danbury, CT: Children's Press, 2003.

Kendell, Patricia. *Tigers*. Chicago: Raintree, 2002.

Web Sites

To find out more about charities that help tigers, visit their Web sites:

WWF: www.worldwildlife.org

Save the Tiger: www.savethetigerfund.org

Glossary

Asia   largest continent in the world

carnivore   animal that eats meat from other animals

continent   large area of land divided into different countries

cub   baby tiger

extinct   when all the animals in a species die out and the species no longer exists

female   animal that can become a mother when it grows up. Women and girls are female people.

habitat   place where plants and animals grow and live. A forest is a type of habitat.

mammal   animal that feeds its baby with the mother's milk and has some hair on its body

mate   what male and female animals do to make babies

poacher   someone who hunts animals when it is against the law to do so

reserve   area of land where animals are protected and their habitat is looked after

species   group of animals that can have babies together

WWF charity that helps endangered species. It is also called the World Wildlife Fund.

Index